The Face of Christ

An amazing story of loss, forgiveness and restoration
found in a simple line drawing of the life of Jesus.

Look to the LORD
and his strength;
seek his face always.
Psalm 105:4

William & Warren Press Inc.
1200 Paint Rock Road
Kingston, TN 37763

Library of congress Cataloging-in-Publication Data
Castillo, Joe;

    ISBN 0-9652007-7-8
    1. Non-Fiction
    2. Biography
    3. Religion

Dewey System – Non-fiction: Short Stories

Printed in the USA

To my father
José Vito Castillo

"Joe, I think you should be an artist,"
was the last thing he said to me.
The best, the most beloved man
I have ever known.

Acknowledgements

I enjoy thanking people.
These are just a few of those who were a part
of the story of the 'Face of Christ.'
My mother who gave me
a love of books and the arts.
I owe much gratitude to Mary
who knew how to forgive.
My children José and Maria
who had to put up with working for me
when they didn't want to,
and endured being 'on the road'.
John Stone the Pastor who prodded me to
do the very first drawing at
Berean Bible Church in Knoxville, TN.
I thank the many people who
believed in my artwork and pruchased it
when I didn't beleive in it myself.
Lyle and Leigh Harris who have
a print of everything I have ever done.
Debbie, Yulan and Dolly
for editing and proofing the manuscript.
Any misteaks that didn't get corrected
are not there fault.
Paul Cowell who encouraged and
inspired me when I was discouraged.
Thank you to all my wonderful and loyal
fans who have motivated me
with your kind words.
Most of all I am in debt to
Cindy.
The cheerful hobbit with a servants' heart
that has traveled the latest part
of this journey with me.

Table of Contents:

An Amazing Story

It is hard to believe that a simple drawing can change someone's life, but it can. I am writing the story of how this illustration changed my life and how it has touched lives all around the globe.

As a commercial artist my work was measured by its quality and by what I got paid. The money really mattered. When I didn't get paid, it chewed up my insides, kept me awake nights, and robbed me of peace. Although I was a Christian, my world still pretty much revolved around me: who I was, and how much I made.

Christmas 1980. My pastor, John Stone had asked me to do a 'Chalk Talk' as part of our Church's Christmas program. This sort of drawing required chalks and a special lighted easel which I didn't have. So I tried to figure out what to do. Magic Markers and rolls of paper were part of a commercial artist's tools, so that became my medium. The drawing was to be done as line art, but I needed an image that would capture the audience's interest. A Christmas drawing had to start from the story of Christ's birth. The ending had to be special. Reading the scriptures in preparation, I realized that the various passages created a composite picture of Christ. The concept that grew out of this idea was to combine small drawings which, when completed, formed His face. God's gift of inspiration took over, and I didn't even recognize it. The hours I invested turned into days and then weeks. I drew it as large as I could reach on a four-foot by eight-foot easel, so it would be visible to a large group.

The program went smoothly and the elements combined cleverly to form the 'Face of Christ.' As I completed the final lines and stepped out of the way, a collective gasp swept across the auditorium. The impact produced a much greater response than I expected. Many people afterward asked if they could get copies. I didn't want to spend any more time on the piece, but enthusiastic friends persuaded me to do a small inked version and make prints available. To my surprise people willingly paid me for it. Now my clever drawing had value! Still, in the 'Face of Christ' I could only see a clever drawing. The only worth it had was financial.

Lonnie,* who was one of my regular customers, owned a company that created simulated marble plaques with etched illustrations and quotations on them. I drew wild animals, boat scenes, and calligraphy sayings for him. Over time he had become not just a customer but also a friend. Because he attended a local church, we had occasionally conversed about our mutual faith. A few months after the Christmas program, he asked if I had any artwork to include in his new line of religious products. I showed him 'The Face of Christ.' He didn't seem very impressed.

9

* Some of the names have been changed out of deference to those in the story.

"Why don't you let me produce some of these?" he asked. "We have to sell about a thousand of them to cover the cost of making the original die, then if we sell more I'll pay you royalties."

Lonnie always seemed straightforward and honest, so I nodded in agreement and left it at that. I really didn't think the drawing would sell. If it did, I certainly would welcome the income. Right then I had no idea that God intended to use my drawing in a totally different and more powerful way.

That summer, with the discovery of a small lump in my wife's right breast, we plunged into a flood of cancer treatments, doctors and red ink. We had no insurance. As summer slipped into fall, my wife Mary struggled with the harsh side effects of chemo treatments and I grappled with overwhelming medical bills. Christmas, for us, and our two young children, promised gloom and empty stockings. When the weather turned cold we decided to take our family walks at the Mall. We were just looking, not Christmas shopping. Walking through the doors of the main entrance on Saturday evening, I received an incredible shock. There stood a full-sized display, covered with marble plaques of the 'Face of Christ!' Wow! There they were, and all had my name on them! I just stood there with my mouth open. We found the same display in the other major department stores, and in the Christian Bookstore, and one in the Mall concourse!

Monday morning at eight o'clock sharp, I called my friend. I had never heard him so excited! He told me my artwork had become the best selling item in their entire line! It was selling like crazy all over the country!

"They are selling so fast we can't keep up with the demand!" he blurted out excitedly. Without really thinking, I asked, "Roughly how much would that add up to in royalties?"

Silence on the other end of the phone sent a chill through my heart.

"Royalties?" He asked.

"Yes, royalties! You said if you sold over a thousand, you would pay me royalties."

Another pause; then, "Oh yes, royalties . . . um, we are getting this all on computer and so I don't have an exact count, but I'll call you back."

With the chill now freezing solid, I hung up the phone. No call came. On Friday I called him and was not able to get him on the phone, so I decided to stop by his office on the following Monday, the week of Christmas. Cordially, he made a point to show me that he had copyrighted the work and displayed the legal documents that went with it. When I asked again about the royalties, he gave me a blank look.

"I don't recall us ever discussing royalties."

Stunned, almost unable to breathe, I stepped out into the cold winter sun. It shed no warmth, and couldn't melt the cold anger forming in my heart. After several attempts to reason with him, and numerous phone calls, he refused to see or speak to me. Christmas slipped past like an unwanted frost. What made it even worse were the excited phone calls from friends in California or Florida telling me how they had seen or purchased my artwork. I could answer only with a terse, "Oh,… great." If they asked questions I would say I didn't want to talk about it. Every word or thought about the 'Face of Christ' spilled bile into my system and bitterness into my soul.

Not everybody understood my problem. As a Bible believing Christian, I wanted to obey the passage that admonished me not to take a Christian brother to court (I Corinthians 6:1-8). I faced a dilemma of God's making, but refused to let Him provide the solution. As my wife struggled with the disease in her body, I struggled with the disease in my heart.

It looked as if this story was going to be one of total loss. My brave wife lost her battle with cancer and went on to be with Christ. I lost out on making perhaps millions of dollars on my artwork. My confidence in God's goodness had suffered a serious blow and I was at risk of losing my faith. But still the 'Face of Christ' kept showing up to torment me in my loss.

After one especially long and sleepless night I was compelled to call out to God. "Look God, You knew all about this before it came into my life. You knew about my wife's cancer, You knew about the stolen artwork. You knew about our financial need. Now, You know how this is eating at me from the inside out and You need to give me the desire and the power to forgive Lonnie."

He reminded me of some very pointed passages in scripture. In Matthew 18:21-35 forgiveness became a big issue with Peter.
"How often should I forgive my brother," he asked. "As many as seven times?"
Christ in response tells him the parable of the man who was forgiven a debt of somewhere around ten million dollars only to go out and have a friend, who owed him a few bucks, thrown into prison. The Master hears about this injustice and calls him in to tell him, "You evil servant! I forgave you that tremendous debt because you pleaded with me. Shouldn't you have mercy on your fellow servant, just as I had mercy on you?" Matthew 18:32,33

The implication was clear. God had forgiven me scores of times for multiple offenses. Should I not be able to forgive my brother this one? Not only had God forgiven me, but He also left an example of how forgiveness should be lived out. Christ was brutalized, being totally innocent, and still found place in his heart for forgiving even those who treated him the worst. "This suffering is all part of what God has called you to. Christ, who suffered for you, is your example. Follow in his steps." 1 Peter 2:21

This was the 'what-would-Jesus-do' principle. Christ forgave those who abused and mistreated Him. We should do the same. Grudgingly, I agreed with God. "OK, I have to forgive. Can you help me out here?" I knew I had to be the initiator and I needed the power to do that. As I demonstrated my willingness to obey God on the outside, the power of His spirit began changing me inside.

God made very clear that the real issue had nothing to do with money or health or even life. If God wanted me to have money, He could have me receive an inheritance, or win a sweepstakes. If God had wanted to heal my wife He could have answered any one of a thousand prayers for her. No, not life or health or money; the issue I faced had to do with control. Who was really in control of my family, my possessions, my abilities, my money? Who brought life or health or blessing or testing into my life, and to whom should I look for my needs? The struggle lasted long into the night. Like Jacob, I had argued with God until the dark hours right before dawn. Finally with humility, I bowed before God and released my anger. I surrendered my artwork, my talents, my wife's death, and my financial difficulties. I gave Him back complete control. I finally let it go. What I saw as a total loss, God saw as an opportunity to bring life. I asked God for the strength to forgive.

God answered my prayer.

One week later came the first evidence that God could work in ways I did not understand. A friend introduced me to the owner of a Christian bookstore. When she heard my name she asked if I had drawn the 'Face of Christ.' Expecting the now common surge of bitterness, I answered that I had, but surprisingly felt a sense of peace.

"Let me tell you what happened just two weeks ago," she said, her face glowing with enthusiasm. "I own a Christian bookstore in Gatlinburg, TN. A customer came browsing through my store and eventually stopped in front of one of the plaques with your drawing. Suddenly I noticed she began to cry. Waiting until she regained her composure, I watched as she took the artwork off the wall and brought it to the cash register. Very curious at her emotional reaction, I asked if she had been moved by the artwork. With tears still in her eyes she answered."

"I don't know what happened. I have been running away from Christ for so many years now, but when I looked into this face and saw all the details of Christ's sacrifice for me, I had to come back to Jesus."

Now I had tears in my eyes. Slowly I awakened to the realization that in some way I could not understand, God could use my artwork to touch people's lives. He could bring life out of death. He could bring hope out of loss. He was the God of resurrection. My payment did not come in dollars, but in spiritual currency that would last for eternity. Since that day I have received hundreds of calls, letters and visits from people deeply affected by this drawing and God's work in their lives.

One couple on the verge of divorce had their marriage restored by the love of Christ. It was the small plaque on their mantelpiece that helped them understand that love. Many more moving stories have followed. The artwork seemed to bring hope to so many. What a great encouragement that was to me!

The company in Knoxville continued to manufacture the plaques and sell them. More than twenty years, hundreds of thousands of plaques and millions of dollars without paying me any royalties. But I continued to hear the amazing stories of people who had been impacted by the artwork.

One of the things that struck me every time I looked at the original drawing was that I knew it was not complete.

The Original Drawing of the 'Face of Christ'

Seek the Lord and His Strength; Seek His Face Continually. Psalm 105:4

One day sitting in my studio I examined again the 'Face of Christ' etched into the plaque that reminded me of anger, frustration and death. Suddenly I knew what was missing. The original drawing did not include the resurrection of Christ. I had left Him hanging on the cross: that cross, which to me seemed to represent failure, defeat and death. While faith in Him brings life, hope and resurrection. Grabbing paper and pencils I began again to redraw Christ's face and the story of His life that put it together. For three days I worked almost without rest. When I was finally done the completed image included many new elements. The most important was that of the empty tomb. HE IS ALIVE! Jesus did not come to just die and leave us without hope. He came to live again! Death was not the end, and this life full of tears is not the final story. The reality of life beyond the grave in a place where there will be no tears. He also forgave us so that we could forgive others.

The drawing had been revived and I thought perhaps God would be able to use the new artwork. God had also given me a new start. Putting my career in advertising behind me, I closed my business and enrolled in Seminary. This would give me an opportunity to serve in ministry. At this crossroads God also brought a wonderful new wife named Cindy into my life. Her patient encouragement prompted me to not leave my artwork behind. A friend helped design a web site where a few of the new prints began selling. But God still had a plan in mind for the original drawing of the 'Face of Christ'.

On February fifteenth 2004, without any advertising, the web site which had not produced much attention, suddenly began to register a huge increase in hits. The orders began to come in at a pace that made February the biggest month in sales ever! As sales continued to climb, people placing orders began telling us that they had received an e-mail containing an image of the 'Face of Christ'. The e-mail just had the cryptic message: "Look closely at the details in this drawing." Finally a friend sent the e-mail to me. Somebody had scanned the original plaque and passed it on to a friend who had passed it to a few more friends and…. We began hearing from and getting orders from people literally around the world. Thousands, maybe millions of people have received the e-mail. The persistent ones would see my name on the artwork and do a web search and find my modest web site. Now the stories really started to come in.

In the same way that the 'Face of Christ' artwork combined individual drawings to form the face, the elements of how God was working in the lives of others began filling in the details of this amazing chronicle. Every life is a story. In ways both small and great, our story impacts the lives and stories of others. My drawing was becoming a thread in the tapestry of other tales.

A young Christian woman had been praying for a number of years that her unbelieving husband would begin to take an interest in Christ. She found a printed copy of the artwork in the trash can at her office and asked the secretary about it. She was told that it had come in on an e-mail and her secretary had made multiple copies for her friends. At home she did a search on her computer and found the artwork on the web site. She was so intrigued she called her husband over to see it. The husband then became fascinated and he told his wife to call me and order two prints of the drawing.

Gail in Houston, TX told me this story. She worked in a real estate office in a rather seedy section of town. On a cold winter morning almost two years earlier a ragged, dirty homeless man shuffled in to her office. Bloodshot eyes, unshaved face and unkempt hair pegged him as a transient. As he approached Gail's desk he began rummaging through his tattered pockets and finally produced a much folded, dog-eared piece of paper that he handed to Gail. "Do you think you could make a few copies of this for me?" came his raspy, whispery voice. Gail reached across her desk to take the paper. On it was the drawing of the 'Face of Christ. "I give copies to the guys on the street," he went on, "and then I tell them about Jesus." Gail, a recovering alcoholic herself, immediately choked up and nodded her head affirmatively.

"I gave him ten copies and he still drops in about every two weeks and gets a few more," Gail told me. "I'm sure that three or four hundred copies of your artwork have been distributed around Houston's homeless population by this raggedy evangelist."

Summer approached that year and the story continued. One morning the phone rang in my studio and a man named John introduced himself. He owned a bridal shop and gift boutique in St. Louis, Missouri. As a committed Christian he had purchased a large plaque of the 'Face of Christ' to hang in his gift shop. Interested customers had asked about it and he had often used it to open a door to explain the Gospel and to lead people to Christ. As he finished telling me his story I was stunned by what he said next.
"Joe, people that appreciated your drawing and were touched by it, wanted to purchase a copy for themselves. I've been selling the plaques for more than twelve years. But I can't order them anymore. The company making them went out of business!"

According to him, the man who had been manufacturing the plaques for more than twenty years had developed cancer and closed his business.

As my wife Cindy and I headed south for our vacation we slowed down in Knoxville, TN and pulled off the interstate to drive by the factory that I knew so well. This was a place that held such bitter memories from so many years before. We pulled into the office parking lot and saw a closed sign on the door. The loading dock looked neglected and a large dumpster stood by the garage door entrance. Climbing the steps to peer into the small glass window of the warehouse door brought me above the level of the dumpster. The lids were open and I glanced in. The image was surrealistic. For a long moment I could do nothing but gape at one of the strangest sights I had ever seen. Covering the bottom five or six inches of the dumpster were hundreds of plaques all bearing the 'Face of Christ' drawing. Cracked, chipped, broken, they were the damaged discards of a business that had lived off the profits of that artwork for more than twenty-five years.

The thought that struck me was how futile our lives become when we discard the only One who can give us hope for the future. How many people have been given the opportunity to follow the Savior and at some point in their lives decided to toss Him out? How many times, by my own decisions or actions, have I done that very thing? From devotion to dumpster. I wish I had taken a picture.

The reality was that I did not even own one of the old plaques anymore because of the memories it triggered. So I climbed down into the dumpster and picked out a few plaques that were not too broken, wiped them off on my blue jeans and returned to my car. There was a phone number on the office door, that I assumed belonged to Lonnie. A strange compulsion that I assume was the prompting of God urged me to call. The voice on the phone was recognizable. As I gave my name there was the same strained, awkward silence on the line I had heard so many years before. But things were very different now. I stepped into the silence and began to reassure Lonnie of how everything had changed.

"Hi Lonnie, I want you to know that everything is fine. I just called because I heard that business was not going well and that you had been sick. If it's alright we wanted to pray for you." Some of the tension eased and he shared with me about how he had gotten overextended, and after receiving the cancer diagnosis, decided to close the business. We shared a few more words and I comforted him with the reminder that God was good and had a purpose for everything. I assured him of our prayers and hung up.

Lonnie was part of the story too. For the next hundred miles down the road Cindy and I kept shaking our heads at the unbelievable irony of this strange situation.

Many months later another phone call added the next chapter to this already unbelievable saga. Terry from Powell Auction Realty in Knoxville, Tennessee informed me that Lonnie's business had filed for bankruptcy. Everything was to be auctioned off. He was calling to notify me of the sale and asked if I was interested in any of the assets. Just out of curiosity I asked him to fax me an itemized list. It arrived with an approximate current market value for each item. One page listed all the artwork that Lonnie had used over the years. Each drawing was valued at $250.00. All of them, except the 'Face of Christ.' The current market value was listed at $50,000.00! I almost fell off my chair!

The auction was scheduled for Saturday, May 21st at 9:00 am. I decided to go. The crazy idea of buying back the rights to my own artwork started forming in my mind.

"What if the bidding went higher than I could afford?" "What if someone else bought the rights and started producing the plaque again?" What if ...." The scenarios were endless. My experience with auctions was nil. It made me nervous. In reality the outcome of the auction really didn't matter. God promises that *"all things will work out for good to those who love Him." Romans 8:28.* But it would still be nice to have it back.

Pulling in to the parking area, seeing a mass of people, and the huge warehouse full of glitzy cars, trucks, tractors, boats and motor homes gave me a bit of perspective on my insignificant little item. The original artwork and copyright assignments comprised a pathetic little pile of framed prints, a cardboard box and a three ring binder of legal documents. No one was going to bid on it. The auctioneer was bellowing some final instructions over a headset microphone. It was 9:00 o'clock. My item was the very first one.

"Ten, dollars, do I hear ten?" I nodded. It jumped to twenty. Somebody was bidding against me! Then fifty, a hundred, two hundred! I swallowed. My heart started beating fast and I whispered a prayer under my breath. Three hundred! Three fifty! I only had five hundred dollars in my checking account. What was I thinking? Finally it stalled. The last bid had been 330. The auctioneer looked at me, "335"? I nodded. A pause... "Sold!" It was over. I breathed a sigh of relief. The crowd moved on. They didn't realize what had just happened. They couldn't know the *real* value of that simple drawing.

There is a wonderful story that Sunday School teachers and Children's workers have told for years. I didn't hear it until I was an adult but even so, the profound Biblical truth it contained moved me to tears. There are many versions of this story and one of the great artists of our time, Ron Dicianni, has done a wonderful painting of it called "The boy who lost his boat." This is the version as I remember it.

The most important thing Chris remembered about his father was that he built boats. A small shed behind the house still held the smell of cedar and hardwoods, everything covered with a coating of sawdust. The worn tools belonging to his father, seemed to fit well in his small hands. It was there that he began to build a tribute to his father's memory. A small model replica of a fine ocean-going sloop slowly began to take shape. Rather than spend time doing the other things young boys did, Tom spent his time working on his boat. After long, laborious months of work the fine miniature yacht was ready. From the stern to the bowsprit, rudder, sails, and rigging were perfect to the last detail. It really was a labor of love.

Designed to actually sail, young Chris had to take it out on the waters of the river nearby. Bright blue sky and a spanking breeze made it a perfect day. The boat performed with all the precision with which it was made and it was a delight to young Chris. Then a different wind began to blow. Clouds rolled in and the sloop, veering in the wrong direction, was taken out into the fast current beyond his reach. Chris chased the boat for a long way before he finally lost sight of it around a bend. For weeks he searched downstream finally, deciding that it was really gone. He was broken hearted.

Months later Chris was riding his bike home from school and passed an old antique shop on the edge of town. There in the window was his boat! It was a little worn looking but he recognized every detail he had put into its making. Rushing in to the store, he breathlessly shouted to the old man that owned the store.

"That's my boat, that's my boat! Mister, can I have my boat back!?"

"Well, hold on now" the old man answered. "How do I know that this is your boat?"

"I made it, I made it myself," the boy sputtered. "That is my boat!"

"That is all well and good," the shopkeeper said, "but somebody sold me that boat and I have to get my money out of it. You might have made it but you lost it and if you want it back I'll have to get fifty dollars for it."

The boy was appalled at the price that the old man was asking but he was determined to get his boat back.

"You hold that boat for me. It is mine and I will be back for it!" he told the old man with passion in his voice.

Delivering papers, mowing lawns, running errands and anything else a young boy could do to earn money consumed Chris' life for the summer. Finally the day came when he clanked an old coffee can down on the counter in the antique store and said,

"Here it is Mister, fifty dollars."
Solemnly the storekeeper counted out the rumpled bills and coins until the total was reached.

"Fifty dollars it is then. The boat is yours." Reaching into the cluttered display window he lifted the graceful sloop out and handed it to the eager little boy. As the door jingled on his way out, Chris clutched the boat to his chest and with great emotion in his voice, the shopkeeper heard him say; "Now little boat, you are twice mine. First I made you, then I bought you back!"

Twice his! That is exactly what Christ did for us. First He made us and enjoyed our company. Then He lost us and finally He bought us back with His own death on the cross to ransom us from the penalty of sin. We also are twice His.

As I write this I have one of the old original plaques sitting on my desk. It is such a poignant reminder that God writes all the stories. Every detail in every life, fits into the whole. Nothing is wasted, nothing is unnecessary. When life seems unfair, when tragedy strikes, when we have been wronged, we need to trust Him. His forgiveness is marvelous and we are urged to forgive those who have wronged us. God is always at work putting the separate parts together. He is combining our individual lives into the likeness of Christ. Some day when the story is completed, He will right all wrongs and every story entrusted to Him will have a happy ending.

Most of all I am reminded that we are His artwork. His handiwork. His masterpiece. He created us, formed us and then when we were lost to Him He bought us back. We are his twice.

And the new drawing? Well, can you believe that the last chapter has not been written yet. In 2004 I signed a contract with one of the world's largest Christian gift manufacturers to make and market the new plaques.

The stories continue to come in. I am still amazed! It is really just a simple illustration but the power of God is at work through this drawing producing miracles.

If you would like to be a part of this story, toward the end of this book is an explanation of how the Face of Christ drawing can be used to explain the good news to those who need to hear it.

Now you can read the scriptures that inspired the drawing and just some of the stories of how God has used it in peoples' lives.

Chapter One
Unexpected Difficulties

All returned to their own towns to register for this census. And because Joseph was a descendant of King David, he had to go to Bethlehem in Judea, David's ancient home. He traveled there from the village of Nazareth in Galilee. He took with him Mary, his fiancée, who was obviously pregnant by this time. And while they were there, the time came for her baby to be born. She gave birth to her first child, a son. She wrapped him snugly in strips of cloth and laid him in a manger, because there was no room for them in the village inn. That night some shepherds were in the fields outside the village, guarding their flocks of sheep. Suddenly, an angel of the Lord appeared among them, and the radiance of the Lord's glory surrounded them. They were terribly frightened, but the angel reassured them. "Don't be afraid!" he said. "I bring you good news of great joy for everyone! The Savior—yes, the Messiah, the Lord—has been born tonight in Bethlehem, the city of David! And this is how you will recognize him: You will find a baby lying in a manger, wrapped snugly in strips of cloth!" Luke 2:2-12

Joe Castillo

19

Chapter One
Unexpected Difficulties

How would you react to finding yourself in trouble that you did not expect; a difficulty that was no fault of your own? A young teenage girl suddenly discovers she is pregnant. Her family is sure to disown her. At the very least she will be ostracized, at worst she could be dragged outside the town where she lived, by the people that have known her all her life, and stoned to death. That was the penalty she faced. She knew there was nothing she had done to get pregnant. When she finally pulls together the courage to tell her boyfriend, he wants to dump her and run.

It is at this fearful and terrifying moment that God intervenes. "Gabriel appeared to her and said, "Greetings, favored woman! The Lord is with you!" Confused and disturbed, Mary tried to think what the angel could mean. "Don't be frightened, Mary," the angel told her, "for God has decided to bless you! You will become pregnant and have a son, and you are to name him Jesus. He will be very great and will be called the Son of the Most High. And the Lord God will give him the throne of his ancestor David. And he will reign over Israel forever; his Kingdom will never end!" Luke 1:28-32

And to the fearful boyfriend God speaks as well. "An angel of the Lord appeared to him in a dream. "Joseph, son of David," the angel said, "do not be afraid to go ahead with your marriage to Mary. For the child within her has been conceived by the Holy Spirit. And she will have a son, and you are to name him Jesus, for he will save his people from their sins. All of this happened to fulfill the Lord's message through his prophet:
"Look! The virgin will conceive a child! She will give birth to a son, and he will be called Immanuel (meaning, God is with us)."
When Joseph woke up, he did what the angel of the Lord commanded. He brought Mary home to be his wife," Matthew 1:20-24

This young couple found themselves at what seemed to be the lowest point in their lives, having a baby in a stable. Mary holds their perfect little newborn. Joseph, his hand on her shoulder, looks on. A patient ox stands by and a lamb lies at their feet beside the manger where the little child would be laid.

A terrifying situation that seemed ready to crush the young couple was transformed into a defining moment in their lives. What they thought would ruin them brought eternal joy!

The Story

My name is Seth. I didn't know that I would be in prison as soon as I turned twenty-one. To celebrate my birthday, I jumped in a car with three other guys that I didn't know very well. They just wanted to party and go out for a joy ride... so I thought. I was waiting in the car while two of the guys ran into a convenience store to buy a case of beer. Suddenly, something went wrong. The two in the store had tried to rob the clerk at gunpoint. The gun went off. They ran back to the car and jumped in. The driver screeched off trying to get away. When we were finally caught, the four of us discovered that the clerk was pronounced D.O.A. at the local hospital. I was tried and convicted as an accessory to the murder and given ten years behind bars in an Idaho prison. I was very depressed and very angry at getting convicted for something I didn't do.

It was at this fearful and terrifying moment that God intervened. What Seth thought would ruin him, brought him eternal hope.

"After almost a year I was invited to a Christian gathering in the prison called 'Kairos.' As I sat in the chapel during the first session I could not take my eyes off a drawing that had been brought by the volunteers as a gift to the prison chapel. It was the drawing of the 'Face of Christ'. During the first break one of the other prisoners who was a Christian invited me to the front of the Chapel to see the drawing closer.

That is when the real impact hit. He began to show me the details in the drawing. As he did he explained the Gospel of Christ. The story of how Christ had been born, how He chose His disciples. How He fed the multitude, then how he was rejected and prayed for us in the garden. I saw how He was arrested, beaten even though he was totally innocent! He then had to carry His cross to be crucified when he did nothing wrong! I heard how he forgave those that had done him wrong. I was angry at everyone in the system. I knew it was wrong. I had lots of other things that I had done wrong. This guy explained how Christ could forgive me for my sin, and how I could forgive everyone I was mad at.

That day looking at that picture, I accepted Christ as my Savior.

Now He is helping me change my life and forgive everybody.

Seth

A Star in the Heavens

Jesus was born in the town of Bethlehem in Judea, during the reign of King Herod. About that time some wise men from eastern lands arrived in Jerusalem, asking, "Where is the newborn king of the Jews? We have seen his star as it arose, and we have come to worship him." Herod was deeply disturbed by their question, as was all of Jerusalem. He called a meeting of the leading priests and teachers of religious law. "Where did the prophets say the Messiah would be born?" he asked them. "In Bethlehem," they said, "for this is what the prophet wrote:

'O Bethlehem of Judah,
     you are not just a lowly village in Judah,
  for a ruler will come from you
        who will be the shepherd for my people Israel.'"

Then Herod sent a private message to the wise men, asking them to come see him. At this meeting he learned the exact time when they first saw the star. Then he told them, "Go to Bethlehem and search carefully for the child. And when you find him, come back and tell me so that I can go and worship him, too!" After this interview the wise men went their way. Once again the star appeared to them, guiding them to Bethlehem. It went ahead of them and stopped over the place where the child was. When they saw the star, they were filled with joy! Matthew 2:1-10

22

Chapter 2
The Star in the Heavens

When God wanted to announce to the world that a *"child would be born and a son would be given,"* He started with a sign. Long before Mary had any knowledge of the coming Messiah, a sign in the heaven appeared. It was a star. A star that was brighter than other stars and apparently pointed in the direction of the tiny town of Bethlehem. It appeared to the wise men in the east. King Herod questioned the Wise Men about the exact time the star was first seen to fix an accurate date for the birth of the child.

"We have seen his star as it arose, and we have come to worship him." Herod was deeply disturbed by their question, as was all of Jerusalem. Then Herod sent a private message to the wise men, asking them to come see him. At this meeting he learned the exact time when they first saw the star." Matthew 2:1,7

Some have suggested that the bright object in the sky was the conjunction of Saturn and Jupiter in the constellation of Pisces. Others suggest that it was a comet or a 'nova' showing up at just the right time. Still others contend that it was a miraculous appearance of a divine star for the specific purpose of guiding the wise men to the newborn child. Whatever method God used, it was intended to point people to Christ. The Wise Men were led to Him, the shepherds sought Him out, and King Herod, even if for all the wrong reasons, became aware of the Christ Child because of the star.

The Story

"My husband is not a believer. He is also not easily impressed. I am always trying to interest him in spiritual things. But here is what happened. As I was working on a project in the copy room at my church I saw a copy of the e-mail the 'Face Of Christ' in the wastebasket. It was like a sign. I picked it up and mentioned it to the secretary, who told me she had received it on an e-mail from a friend. At my request She then wrote down my e-mail address and sent it to my computer."

"I felt the need to research the artwork and found your web site. When I started scrolling over the pictures and getting scripture references, I was awestruck. I called my husband down to the basement where I was, and he thought it was so cool that he told me to order the two prints of the 'Face of Christ'. That almost knocked me over because he is pretty tight with his money and not easily impressed. The artwork made quite an impression and I wanted you to know about it. You have not heard the last from us.
Thank you so much for touching my heart and pointing my husband toward Christ."

Sincerely,
Susan

Proclaiming the Message

Suddenly, an angel appeared among the radiance of the rounded them. They were the angel reassured them. "Don't be afraid!" he of the Lord them, and Lord's glory surterribly frightened, but said. "I bring you good news of great joy for everyone! The Savior – yes, the Messiah, the Lord – has been born tonight in Bethlehem, the city of David! And this is how you will recognize him: You will find a baby lying in a manger, wrapped snugly in strips of cloth!" Suddenly, the angel was joined by a vast host of others – the armies of heaven – praising God:

"Glory to God in the highest heaven, and peace on earth to all whom God favors." When the angels had returned to heaven, the shepherds said to each other, "Come on, let's go to Bethlehem! Let's see this wonderful thing that has happened, which the Lord has told us about." Luke 2:8-15

Chapter 3
Proclaiming The Message

Oh, the privilege of being able to bring good news to people! It would be a great job to be someone like Ed McMahon, showing up on people's doorsteps to tell them they had won ten million dollars. We like to be bearers of glad tidings. I remember my sister dancing around the house with a letter that had arrived announcing my acceptance to Art School. She had nothing to do with getting me accepted, but she really had fun when telling me about it!

Sharing good news is telling your roommate that a perfumed letter is in the mailbox; rejoicing with your expectant wife that it is a girl; just what she wanted; trumpeting to the fans that their team won the game; proclaiming a raise; handing out a bonus; shouting "Hey kids we are going to Disneyworld!"

All of those pronouncements, even Ed McMahon's ten million dollars, are things that won't last forever. They are the stuff of temporary joy. What the angels showed up announcing was something eternal. The Chosen one, the Savior was to be born. What they were proclaiming was the truth that all people could be forgiven for their sins and would have the hope of an eternal home in heaven. That was great news!

"… the angel reassured them. "Don't be afraid!" he said. "I bring you good news of great joy for everyone! The Savior – yes, the Messiah, the Lord – has been born tonight in Bethlehem, the city of David!" Luke 2:11

The Shepherds also, having heard the great news, started telling everyone about the baby that had been born and the fantastic news the angel had given them.

"They ran to the village and found Mary and Joseph. And there was the baby, lying in the manger. Then the shepherds told everyone what had happened and what the angel had said to them about this child. All who heard the shepherds' story were astonished!" Luke 2:16-18

When you have great news you just can't keep it to yourself.

The Story

"Hello, Joe, my name is John. I am calling from Saint Louis, Missouri, to tell you about how your artwork has impacted my life and the lives of my customers."

John owned a bridal boutique and gift shop. As a committed Christian he had purchased a large plaque of the 'Face of Christ' to hang in the shop. But what happened next was a surprise to him. People walking through his store would stop and begin to scrutinize the details in the drawing. One morning John was arranging merchandise on the shelves when a young woman stopped in front of the plaque and began examining the details.

"This is really intriguing," she said without taking her eyes off the plaque.

"Yes, it has the story of Jesus in his face," John responded.

"Really? I don't know much about that. I never went to church as a kid." This time her eyes flickered towards John and back to the drawing.

"Well look, here is where it starts. Here is the star, and his birth with Mary and Joseph in the stable."

So John began pointing out each illustration and how it related to the good news of Christ's birth, miraculous life, death and resurrection. Then came the part John had not anticipated at all. As he finished, "and so Jesus rose from the dead to prove that our sins were paid for. If we trust in Him we can have forgiveness and know that we will be with Him in heaven."

The young woman turned to face him, her cheeks wet with tears.

"Wow! I never heard that before!"

John was stunned and before he knew it the words were out of his mouth.

"Would you like to trust Christ as your Savior?"

"Yes, I would," the young woman said and bowed her head. In the silence of that sacred moment John felt tears forming in his own eyes. This young woman became a Christian right here, in his own little gift shop.

Speaking Out

Then Jesus returned to Galilee, filled with the Holy Spirit's power. Soon he became well known throughout the surrounding country. He taught in their synagogues and was praised by everyone. When he came to the village of Nazareth, his boyhood home, he went as usual to the synagogue on the Sabbath and stood up to read the Scriptures. The scroll containing the messages of Isaiah the prophet was handed to him, and he unrolled the scroll to the place where it says:

"The Spirit of the Lord is upon me, for he has appointed me to preach Good News to the poor. He has sent me to proclaim that captives will be released, that the blind will see, that the downtrodden will be freed from their oppressors, and that the time of the Lord's favor has come."

He rolled up the scroll, handed it back to the attendant, and sat down. Everyone in the synagogue stared at him intently. Then he said, "This Scripture has come true today before your very eyes!" All who were there spoke well of him and were amazed by the gracious words that fell from his lips. Luke 4:14-22

Chapter 4
Speaking Out

If we listen, God prompts us when to speak out and He gives us opportunities to share His good news. Very unexpected people in unexpected places have been motivated to speak the name of Christ because of difficult situations in their lives. Tragedy is often the catalyst that helps us establish right priorities.

Christ, at the very beginning of His earthly ministry, spoke out in the synagogue reading from the passage in Isaiah where he was appointed to give the good news to hurting people. So many of the stories I have heard concerning the 'Face of Christ' drawing have been those connected with how people were encouraged to speak out during times of hardship to remind people of God's love and provision. Hardship often gives us boldness to speak when we ordinarily would be silent. Difficulties will undoubtedly make others more receptive as well. The good news is often more welcome by the poor and the captives, the blind and the downtrodden.

"The Lord has appointed me to bring good news to the poor. He has sent me to comfort the brokenhearted and to announce that captives will be released and prisoners will be freed. He has sent me to tell those who mourn that the time of the Lord's favor has come." Isaiah 61:1,2

The Story

This was an e-mail I received from a professor at Quillen School of Medicine in Johnson City, Tennessee.

Dear Joe,

A number of years ago, my wife Joyce purchased a print of the 'Face of Christ' as a gift for me. It has been hanging in my office at the medical school since then. Many people, particularly my students, have seen and responded to this image. I have had the opportunity to show them the detail of the work and to explain to them what each of the "pictures" means.

I was diagnosed with leukemia in April, 2002. I am currently in remission after nearly dying from pneumonia as a complication of "too much chemo" a year ago. I praise the Lord every day for the additional time he has given me here to be a servant for Him and to spend with my family. I have been encouraged viewing your print nearly everyday as well. I am semi-retired now working just part-time. But I still have students come in to my office and see your print.

I looked for you online as a result of a young medical student in my office this morning, who saw the 'Face of Christ,' and asked me if you had a web site. She wants to become an oncologist. The image was a great encouragement to her as she struggles with anorexia and getting through her second year of medical school.

Best wishes,

Leo M. Harvill, Ph.D.

A Call to Follow

One day as Jesus was preaching on the shore of the Sea of Galilee, great crowds pressed in on him to listen to the word of God. He noticed two empty boats at the water's edge, for the fishermen had left them and were washing their nets. Stepping into one of the boats, Jesus asked Simon, its owner, to push it out into the water. So he sat in the boat and taught the crowds from there. When he had finished speaking, he said to Simon, "Now go out where it is deeper and let down your nets, and you will catch many fish."

"Master," Simon replied, "we worked hard all last night and didn't catch a thing. But if you say so, we'll try again." And this time their nets were so full they began to tear! A shout for help brought their partners in the other boat, and soon both boats were filled with fish and on the verge of sinking. When Simon Peter realized what had happened, he fell to his knees before Jesus and said, "Oh, Lord, please leave me — I'm too much of a sinner to be around you." For he was awestruck by the size of their catch, as were the others with him. His partners, James and John, the sons of Zebedee, were also amazed. Jesus replied to Simon, "Don't be afraid! From now on you'll be fishing for people!"
Luke 5:10

29

Chapter Five
A Call to Follow

Followers of Christ come from the most unexpected places. It is ironic that some of the first followers Jesus picked were fishermen. What an unlikely place to start. They were the uneducated, the unpolished, rather coarse segment of society. But it was these rough fishermen that Christ challenged to become the seeds of the greatest movement in the history of the world! What is amazing is their willingness to follow the One who called them to change their vocation from fishing for seafood to fishing for men. What motivated them was the reality that 'The Christ' could do things they could not. He was able to change the winds and the tide, He could bring fish into empty nets, He could change human hearts. These rough fishermen had worked all night and not caught anything. At Christ's command they again let down their nets only to find the catch overflowing the nets, the boat, and their limited faith. Even Peter -the most unlikely of them all- was stunned.

"For he was awestruck by the size of their catch, as were the others with him. His partners, James and John, the sons of Zebedee, were also amazed. Jesus replied to Simon, 'Don't be afraid! From now on you'll be fishing for people!' And as soon as they landed, they left everything and followed Jesus." Luke 5:9-11

The Story

"I gave my life to Christ tonight!" were the first words out of her mouth. "I want to follow Him and tell others about Him."

I had just completed a live drawing of the 'Face of Christ' at Mercy Street, a Saturday night recovery ministry held at Chapelwood United Methodist Church in Houston, Texas. This was a ministry designed for those struggling with addictions, compulsive behaviors and dysfunctional lives. Margarite, the young woman standing before me, appeared to be anything but dysfunctional. Beautiful, elegant, styled hair, designer leather purse with the obligatory cell phone clipped to it, and dressed from the pages of a fashion magazine, she could have been a lawyer, Wall Street broker or CEO of her own corporation. But her perfect makeup was now puddled under her eyes and running down her face. As a recovering alcoholic, she longed for real purpose in a life filled with the hectic pursuit of material gain. Three-martini lunches and open-bar corporate business functions had snared her into alcoholic bondage. Through AA she had managed to stay sober for two years, but the emptiness of not having a real purpose for life weighed her down. Now, through that simple drawing she knew what her calling was: being a fisher of people.

Food for the Hungry

After this, Jesus crossed over the Sea of Galilee, also known as the Sea of Tiberias. And a huge crowd kept following him wherever he went, because they saw his miracles as he healed the sick. Then Jesus went up into the hills and sat down with his disciples around him. (It was nearly time for the annual Passover celebration.) Jesus soon saw a great crowd of people climbing the hill, looking for him. Turning to Philip, he asked, "Philip, where can we buy bread to feed all these people?" He was testing Philip, for he already knew what he was going to do. Philip replied, "It would take a small fortune to feed them! Then Andrew, Simon Peter's brother, spoke up. "There's a young boy here with five barley loaves and two fish. But what good is that with this huge crowd?" "Tell everyone to sit down," Jesus ordered. So all of them — the men alone numbered five thousand — sat down on the grassy slopes. Then Jesus took the loaves, gave thanks to God, and passed them out to the people. Afterward he did the same with the fish. And they all ate until they were full. "Now gather the leftovers," Jesus told his disciples, "so that nothing is wasted." There were only five barley loaves to start with, but twelve baskets were filled with the pieces of bread the people did not eat! John 6:1-13

Joe Castill

31

Chapter 6
Food for the Hungry

You don't need much. When you are caught in a situation where the need exceeds your supply, that is where God can step in. Over and over again in times of want I have discovered that God was able to take what little I had to supply my need. He has always been able to multiply the small offering that I gave to him.

Philip was presented with the dilemma of feeding a huge crowd of people. Christ knew that it was beyond his resources and Philip made it known.

"He was testing Philip, for he already knew what he was going to do. Philip replied, 'It would take a small fortune to feed them!" John 6:6,7

That was when Andrew pointed out that they did have something.

"There's a young boy here with five barley loaves and two fish." John 6:8,9

That was when God took over. Because of Andrew's faith and the willingness of a little boy to part with his picnic lunch, a great miracle was performed! More than five thousand people were fed and twelve baskets were left over after everyone ate until they were full!

The Story

One hundred and twenty-five unruly, unchurched teenagers from a rough section of Baton Rouge, Louisiana, were expecting a band and speaker for their evening camp program. It was supposed to be the highlight of the week. There had been a lot of promises about how great this band was. It was strong enticement because teenagers love music. But at the last minute the band canceled! The call came in with the kids already in the auditorium that the band's bus had broken down. There would be no program but there might be a riot.

Quiet, soft-spoken Sister Mary Martha was going to have to break the news. As camp coordinator the buck stopped with her. In her small cubicle of an office she could hear the noise mounting in the auditorium overhead. There was only time for a quick prayer. She reached for her Bible as she headed for what she expected would be the lion's den. The Bible slipped from her fingers and fell to the floor, a folded sheet of paper fluttered out. It was a copy of the 'Face of Christ' artwork that one of the other sisters had printed out from the ubiquitous e-mail. Inspiration struck. A quick stop at the copy machine and it was turned into an overhead transparency, which she carried with trembling hand into the crowded auditorium. As she flipped on the overhead projector she covered all but the beard on the drawing. The noise subsided as she began to speak. "The bus that was bringing the band broke down and they will not be able to be here, but I am going to tell you the most amazing story ever told."

It was at this point that the Sister's eyes began to glisten as she described to me the scene in that auditorium. I still get amazed thinking about what she told me really happened!

She began giving the story of Christ's birth. As soon as she began sliding the paper over to reveal the angels, silence enveloped the room. The kids were spellbound. As each scene appeared the interest increased. By the time she reached the crucifixion scene, sniffling could be heard around the auditorium. The eyes of the drawing were still covered. Almost a full hour had gone by. "You can believe that God really loves you," Sister Mary Martha concluded, " and He has demonstrated that love in Jesus Christ." At that point she slipped the paper off the transparency exposing the completed face. A gasp swept across the room! It was punctuated by 'Wow!' and 'Cool!' And in the intensity of the moment she could only say "let us pray."

Sitting in my studio the Sister concluded her story by saying "You will never know the impact your drawing had on those students! They were still talking about it six months later."

Petitions for God

Then, accompanied by the disciples, Jesus left the upstairs room and went as usual to the Mount of Olives. There he told them, "Pray that you will not be overcome by temptation."

He walked away, about a stone's throw, and knelt down and prayed, "Father, if you are willing, please take this cup of suffering away from me. Yet I want your will, not mine." Then an angel from heaven appeared and strengthened him. He prayed more fervently, and he was in such agony of spirit that his sweat fell to the ground like great drops of blood. At last he stood up again and returned to the disciples, only to find them asleep, exhausted from grief. "Why are you sleeping?" he asked. "Get up and pray. Otherwise temptation will overpower you." Luke 22:39-46

Joe Castillo

Chapter Seven
Petitions for God

God has not answered all my prayers. In fact I would say that many of my most passionate prayers have not produced the result I desired. Wrong motives, sin in my life or confusion about what is the right thing to pray, can be just some of the reasons. I continue to pray, however. I pray now more than I ever have, because on a regular basis God answers a prayer in such a compelling way that it could only have been Him.

"The earnest prayer of a righteous person has great power and wonderful results."
James 5:16

Fervent secret prayers, prayed by sincere, honest people in solitary places, sometimes get answered in the most surprising ways. But God reserves the right to filter our prayers and answer those He chooses. I can trust Him with that. It is the way a good father would delight in giving the most trivial desire but withhold a request that would cause his child harm.

Christ prayed to the Father often. He was our model and in His prayers we can find the best examples in how to pray. He admonished us to pray all the time, even for the simplest things. But not all his prayers were answered. At the darkest point in His life He prayed;

"Father, if you are willing, please take this cup of suffering away from me."

Yet, regardless of the fact that the Father would not answer this prayer, Jesus trusted Him with the outcome.

"Yet I want your will, not mine." Luke 22:42

Compared to this prayer, many of the requests Christ made were insignificant, almost trivial. He prayed and found a coin in the mouth of a fish. He prayed and a thunderstorm blew over. He prayed and a shortage of wine at a wedding was supplied. How trivial is that?

When we pray, God, reserves the right to not grant our request, but no prayer is trivial. Our loving Father delights in even our most childlike desires.

When my son was only five years old, I was trying to teach him how to pray. We were sitting on a log one evening during a family camping trip. As we prayed, I was waxing eloquent, asking God for great things. When it was my son's turn he simply said,

"Dear God, I would like to see a turtle."

The words had no sooner come across his lips than a rustling came up from under the log. Goose bumps crawled up my spine and the hair on the back of my neck stood straight up! Crawling between us was a ten inch box turtle!

The Story

Magdala knew well what it was to pray fervently and not have her prayers answered. Her first child had been born with severe congenital birth defects and for many days she prayed that God would spare the life of her baby boy. But it was not to be. She and her husband embraced the child for only a few moments after he died and then had to let him go. Instead of crushing her faith, Magdala became a woman of prayer. Her Pastor, a good friend of mine, told me later that over the years she had become the prayer warrior of his church.

The way I met Magdala was another one of those inexplicable stories. She worked at St. Joseph Hospital in Lexington, Kentucky as a nurses' aid. One day a newly appointed priest hung a print of the 'Face of Christ' on his office wall. Magdala was captivated. She begged the priest to allow her to make a copy of the artwork. The print had been given to him and he had no idea how to get another one. Reluctantly he allowed her to do that and she took the copy home to show her husband. One day while in the priest's office, she prayed out loud that she could meet the artist who did the drawing. A trivial request perhaps but, that next Sunday evening at the Hispanic service at her church, I walked in to do one of the live drawings. Her Pastor had asked me to come and do the drawing two months earlier! As soon as the service was over she came up to me and said, "I know why you came tonight."

"Oh?" I answered, not knowing what else to say.

"It is because I asked God to meet the artist that did the drawing." And then she told me her surprising story. Magdala now has a signed limited edition print of her very own.

Heavy Burdens

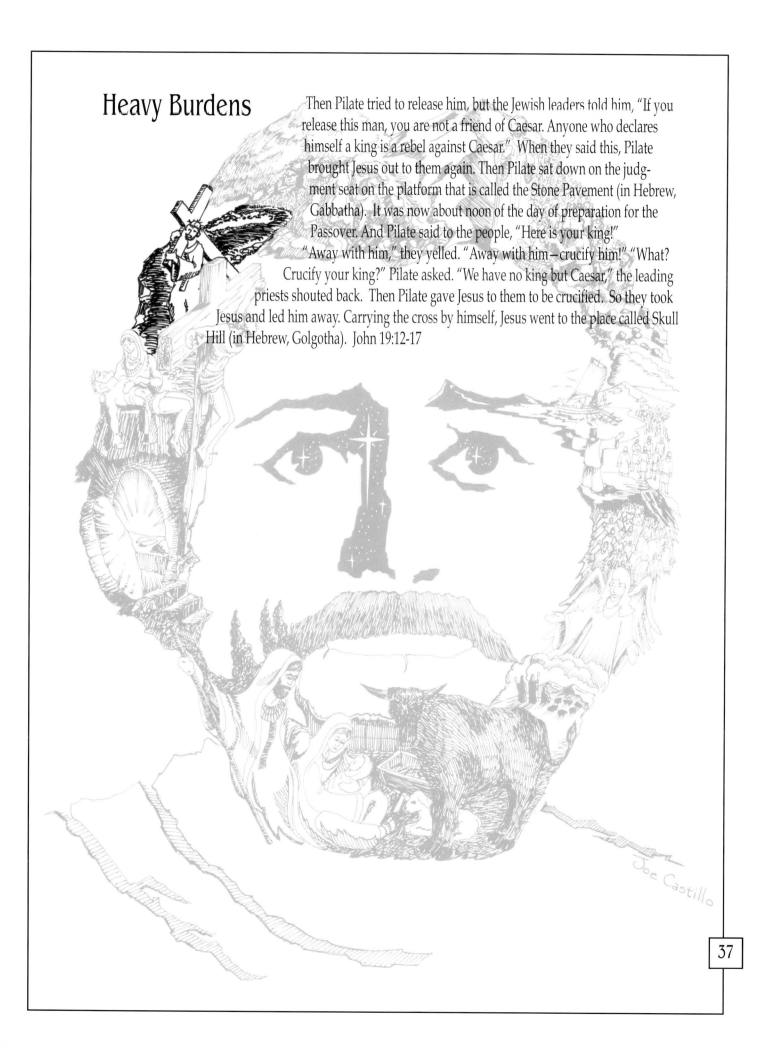

Then Pilate tried to release him, but the Jewish leaders told him, "If you release this man, you are not a friend of Caesar. Anyone who declares himself a king is a rebel against Caesar." When they said this, Pilate brought Jesus out to them again. Then Pilate sat down on the judgment seat on the platform that is called the Stone Pavement (in Hebrew, Gabbatha). It was now about noon of the day of preparation for the Passover. And Pilate said to the people, "Here is your king!"

"Away with him," they yelled. "Away with him—crucify him!" "What? Crucify your king?" Pilate asked. "We have no king but Caesar," the leading priests shouted back. Then Pilate gave Jesus to them to be crucified. So they took Jesus and led him away. Carrying the cross by himself, Jesus went to the place called Skull Hill (in Hebrew, Golgotha). John 19:12-17

Joe Castillo

Chapter Eight
Heavy Burdens

The load seems too heavy to bear. We cry out under the burden, "Oh God, deliver me!" But somehow, if anything, the weight seems to increase.

Some can almost identify with the image of Christ shouldering the cross on a back already bloodied by scourging. Our Lord carried the load longer and farther than seemed possible for human endurance.

"Carrying the cross by himself, Jesus went to the place called Skull Hill." John 19:17

Staggering often, falling at times, He represents all of humankind who are crushed under burdens greater than they can bear. It was undoubtedly this future event that Christ had in mind when he spoke the words:

"Come to me all you who are weary and carry heavy burdens, and I will give you rest. Take my yoke upon you. Let me teach you, because I am humble and gentle, and you will find rest for your souls. For my yoke fits perfectly and the burden I give is light." Matthew 11:28-30

It is at those very times of extreme press, that in Christ we can find peace in the moment and strength for the journey. Looking into His face may not bring immediate relief but it can bring strength and peace. Beth found my web site, read my story of the drawing and sent me this e-mail.

The Story

About 4 years ago, after 27 years of marriage, I went through a horrible divorce from a violent and abusive husband. One week after the divorce, I was driving my car and a tree fell on top of it, crushing the car and me in it. Fortunately my injuries were not severe but it was so discouraging. I tried to be thankful, but felt upset about all I had lost. (my husband, marriage, church family, friends) Our three children have been deeply affected by this, as I'm sure you can understand. The two girls, age 29 today & 23, have had a very difficult time with their dad. Not too long ago our son, age 26 sent me this e-mail containing the picture of Jesus. I am forever grateful to the Lord's strength in his life. He loved this artwork so much he thought it would be an encouragement to me. And it really has. I have found great peace!

Anyway, thank you for your awesome work. I have admired it so. Thank you even more for sharing your story. Really that makes the art even more valuable, as we can see the need for the Lord throughout every aspect of life. We need His love and forgiveness. What an example to us..... that we must likewise forgive the wrongs we've experienced.

Blessings to you.

Sincerely,

Beth Thornburg

Death of A Dream

And they brought Jesus to a place called Golgotha (which means Skull Hill). They offered him wine drugged with myrrh, but he refused it. Then they nailed him to the cross. They gambled for his clothes, throwing dice to decide who would get them. It was nine o'clock in the morning when the crucifixion took place. A signboard was fastened to the cross above Jesus' head, announcing the charge against him. It read: "The King of the Jews." Two criminals were crucified with him, their crosses on either side of his. And the people passing by shouted abuse, shaking their heads in mockery. "Ha! Look at you now!" they yelled at him. "You can destroy the Temple and rebuild it in three days, can you? Well then, save yourself and come down from the cross!" The leading priests and teachers of religious law also mocked Jesus. "He saved others," they scoffed, "but he can't save himself! Let this Messiah, this king of Israel, come down from the cross so we can see it and believe him!" Even the two criminals who were being crucified with Jesus ridiculed him. At noon, darkness fell across the whole land until three o'clock. Then, at that time Jesus called out with a loud voice, "Eloi, Eloi, lema sabachthani?" which means, "My God, my God, why have you forsaken me?" Mark 15:34

Chapter Nine
Death of a Dream

All the way through the Bible we read the histories of God's children having dreams of great things. Almost all of them watched the dream die. Abraham, Moses, David, and Gideon all knew the death of a dream. In the despair of the moment, when all hope seems lost there can be human attempts to salvage the dream. In reality only God can bring about resurrection. Only He can restore the hope that has been lost. All of those in the Old Testament and all of us today can find that hope. God can still use a failure like Moses to lead His children. God can use an impotent, one hundred year-old man to produce children. God can restore lost kingdoms and only He can bring victory out of defeat.

The disciples dreamed of the defeat of the conquering Romans and of establishing a new kingdom. At the crucifixion of Christ all of those dreams were dashed. Death robbed them of hope. That is when God intervened, reviving the dream in a way they never expected. The much greater foe that Christ conquered was death and the Kingdom He established was to last forever. Great hope was reborn.

Here is a story of hope and renewal.

The Story

Julie's hope for a Christian marriage had died. After twelve years her husband Bill refused to go to church or have anything to do with her faith. He had become distant, resentful and angry. Even their ten year old daughter could not get him to have any interest in spiritual things. Julie was sure that any hope for the marriage was dead.

In the spring of 1994 Bill lost his job and came home in a drunken rage. Inside the house he began breaking everything he could get his hands on. He was grabbing and smashing things against the wall. On the mantle rested the marble etching of the 'Face of Christ.' He reached for it. Snatching it up to throw it against the wall, his eyes began to see the details in the face. He had never seen them before. Captivated, he studied the drawing. Then the impact of Christ's love gripped his heart. Slumping to the couch he called to his wife and daughter, who were hiding from his wrath under the bed. They crept fearfully out of the bedroom. Julie couldn't believe her eyes. Bill was sitting on the couch holding the plaque with tears running down his face. Through choked sobs he asked her if she had ever noticed the details. She told him that was why she had purchased it almost ten years earlier. Together they stared at the face and then in tears, held each other and prayed that God would restore their marriage. Bill came to know Christ, and three weeks later they drove all the way down from Virginia to sit in my studio and tell me their story.

Loving Service

Some women were there, watching from a distance, including Mary Magdalene, Mary (the mother of James the younger and of Joseph), and Salome. They had been followers of Jesus and had cared for him while he was in Galilee. Then they and many other women had come with him to Jerusalem. This all happened on Friday, the day of preparation, the day before the Sabbath. As evening approached, an honored member of the high council, Joseph from Arimathea (who was waiting for the Kingdom of God to come), gathered his courage and went to Pilate to ask for Jesus' body. Pilate couldn't believe that Jesus was already dead, so he called for the Roman military officer in charge and asked him. The officer confirmed the fact, and Pilate told Joseph he could have the body. Joseph bought a long sheet of linen cloth, and taking Jesus' body down from the cross, he wrapped it in the cloth and laid it in a tomb that had been carved out of the rock. Then he rolled a stone in front of the entrance. Mary Magdalene and Mary the mother of Joseph saw where Jesus' body was laid. Mark 15:47

Joe Castillo

Chapter Ten
Loving Service

In the three years that Christ traveled the roads of Israel, some took it upon themselves to be His servants. They prepared meals, washed and mended his clothes and sat at His feet to hear Him teach. As He taught on servanthood they learned it the best.

"He who would be greatest among you," Christ taught, *"should be your servant."*
Matthew 23:11

When Jesus finally died, *"Some women were there, watching from a distance, including Mary Magdalene, Mary the mother of James, and Salome. They had been followers of Jesus and had cared for him while he was in Galilee." Mark 15:40*

It is obvious that they steadfastly waited at the cross. No doubt they helped with the preparations for His burial. And when He rose from the dead they were there. Mary Magdalene was one of them, a woman with a bad reputation, who had lived to fulfill her own desires. In Christ Mary had learned to have a servant's heart. With humility she had even stooped to wipe his feet with her hair. She was serving Him as she carried the spices to the tomb. After His resurrection, of all his disciples, Jesus appeared first to her. The very first word spoken after He emerged from the tomb was "Mary."

Mothers do servanthood better than most. They serve their families and children, mostly with a cheerful heart. When the kids get unruly in church, mothers are usually the ones to find a way to keep them interested or take them out of the service.

The Story

"Wow! This morning I was rushing to get to church with my husband and four-year-old son. We rushed to our seats and the service began. Several minutes later my son said that he was thirsty. After several minutes of "I'm thirsty, Mommy," I gave in and took him out to the foyer to get a cup to fill with water. Our church had 'the Face of Christ' and the 'Lord Is My Shepherd' on display in the foyer. My son (an animal lover) immediately spotted the lamb in the 'Lord Is My Shepherd,' and said "Mommy look at Jesus. That lamb was scared so Jesus picked it up and held it so it wouldn't be scared anymore." I couldn't get past Jesus' face in the 'Face of Christ,' the closer I got the more I could see. All I could think or say was Wow! Pain, love, warmth, admiration, acceptance, I felt like you could see so many emotions in his face and eyes. This artwork is beautiful, and had it not been for our thirsty son, I would have missed the whole thing. We usually leave the church through another door, but I made my husband go back out through that door so he could see them too. I looked Joe up on the internet and I feel like I hit a gold mine finding this site. What a blessing this artwork is. Keep up the amazing work, we will be praying for you."

New Life

But very early on Sunday morning the women came to the tomb, taking the spices they had prepared. They found that the stone covering the entrance had been rolled aside. So they went in, but they couldn't find the body of the Lord Jesus. They were puzzled, trying to think what could have happened to it. Suddenly, two men appeared to them, clothed in dazzling robes. The women were terrified and bowed low before them. Then the men asked, "Why are you looking in a tomb for someone who is alive? He isn't here! He has risen from the dead! Don't you remember what he told you back in Galilee, that the Son of Man must be betrayed into the hands of sinful men and be crucified, and that he would rise again the third day?" Then they remembered that he had said this. So they rushed back to tell his eleven disciples —and everyone else—what had happened.
Luke 24:1-9

Joe Castillo

Chapter Eleven
New Life

How would it be to start all over? To erase the past and begin again with a clean slate, a clear conscience. It is wonderful. It is what Christ offers in His death, burial and resurrection. But what happens to those who fall again? Does grace continue to cover the 'bruised reed' or the 'guttering lamp?' Oh I assure you it does! As often as we fail, God is there to lift us up.

"But as people sinned more and more, God's wonderful kindness became more abundant." *Romans 5:20*

This is so evident in the empty tomb. Like forensic experts, our accusers rush to the tomb to find evidence of the crime. There must be a dead body and somebody will be found guilty. But God cleared the evidence away. There can be no charge of guilt to one who is exonerated of a crime. If the prosecuting attorney has nothing to convict us with, then we must be in the clear.

"He has removed our rebellious acts as far away from us as the east is from the west." *Psalms 103:12*

What a blessed assurance. As often as we fall He will lift us up.
"They may trip seven times, but each time they will rise again." Proverbs 24:16
This is the greatest evidence of the Grace of God, that He is able to continually give us new life. To be able to start over not once, not twice, but every single day until He calls us home. We know that *"his mercies begin afresh each day!"* Lamentations 3:23

The Story

Of all the people I know, no one, I mean really no one, has seen more personal failure in their lives than Sandy. She has struggled with every form of addictive substance and behavior that I could name. Having escaped from an abusive family situation she proceeded to make one bad choice after another. Her self-destructive decisions almost ended her life at least three times that I know of, not counting the multiple suicide attempts. My first wife Mary had known her from high school and we had helped her out of various messes over the years. Sometimes I helped willingly, sometimes just because she was my wife's friend, and at times I didn't help at all. Her greatest struggle came in believing that God could continue to forgive her for her multiple failures. Sandy got to know me pretty well over the years too. She has probably seen me at my best and at my worst.

Sandy purchased one of the very first plaques of the 'Face of Christ'. Before I even knew how widely they were selling she called our home to tell us that she had seen it in a store and recognized my name. Those were still the angry days. In that special way that I still don't understand, the image had encouraged her of Christ's continuing love. Over the years she purchased several plaques and gave them away as gifts. When I did the new drawing she began buying prints to give to friends.

I keep losing track of Sandy, yet from time to time she inevitably turns up to order a new supply. What I am reminded of whenever she comes to mind is the incredible overwhelming forgiveness of God.

Sandy, if you ever get a chance to read this, know that you are forgiven by His grace even as I have, and we find that forgiveness in the real face of Jesus.

    joe

How to Share the Good News
Using the 'Face of Christ' Drawing

Remember, my drawing is just that–a drawing of the significant events in the life of Jesus that together portray His face. It is not something to be venerated or considered sacred. It is just a drawing. But like the staff of Moses, God is able to take a very ordinary instrument and perform extraordinary events and even miracles. Using an ordinary wooden stick, imbued with the power of God, Moses was able to change the heart of a brutal king, open a way that was closed, bring life-giving water from a rock, and set His people free.

In a way that I cannot explain, God has used this simple drawing to change hearts, open closed doors, bring living water to those that were thirsty and set people free through the Gospel of Jesus Christ. You have read some of these amazing stories.

With the illustration you now hold in your hand God can use you to help people find freedom!

I began to understand the reality of this a few years ago when John called. You read a little bit of his story in Chapter 3. John was the one that owned the bridal boutique and gift shop. He was the first one that I heard of, other than myself, who had used the 'Face of Christ' artwork to lead someone to Christ.

As I got to know John better over a period of months, I discovered he was not a pastor and had no theological training. He was just a Christian with the desire to have others understand the love of God and the forgiveness found in Christ. The drawing became a valuable tool in capturing the interest of those needing to hear the message. John is still telling the story.

Over the years I had explained the Gospel dozens of times in live-art presentations and have seen many come to Christ. Hearing John's story helped me realize that anyone could point out the elements in the drawing while explaining the good news in a simple, clear and captivating way. It is the Gospel that has the power to touch a place in people's hearts, drawing them to trust Christ!

I have compiled this book to help you use your 'Face of Christ' plaque to inspire others to "Seek His Face." My prayer is that you will find this to be a valuable tool in pointing others to the Savior.

Getting Started
PRAYER

Reaching people with the Gospel is a spiritual process. Opening a conversation with God through prayer is essential in laying the groundwork for conversations with seekers about Christ.

1. Pray that God will give you opportunities to share the good news.
2. Pray for the words to speak as you talk to people about Christ.
3. Pray for those who will hear this message that God would give them receptive hearts.

"The harvest is so great, but the workers are so few. Pray to the Lord who is in charge of the harvest, and ask him to send out more workers for his fields." Luke 10:2

SCRIPTURE

Remember that the word of God is your most powerful tool in sharing the good news. God's word is the "living water," the "bread of life" and the "double-bladed sword" that can slice to the heart, soul and spirit of every individual.

1. Familiarize yourself with many of the scriptures that explain salvation.
2. Memorize key verses so they will come to mind when you need them.
3. Keep a Bible handy for when questions arise and have salvation passages marked.

"For the word of God is full of living power. It is sharper than the sharpest knife, cutting deep into our innermost thoughts and desires. It exposes us for what we really are." Hebrews 4:12

OPPORTUNITIES

Set your plaque in a prominent place in your home or business. This drawing has been proliferated around the internet and has landed in many unsuspecting e-mail boxes. Many thousands of people who don't know the Savior have seen it. Sharing the good news of God's forgiveness can be the most natural, winsome thing you can do if you are just aware of the opportunities God brings you. When people stop to look at your plaque, ask them if they have ever seen that artwork before. Regardless of their answer you can begin pointing out the story of Christ's life.

"Pray that this message is proclaimed as clearly as it should. Live wisely among those who are not Christians, and make the most of every opportunity. Let your conversation be gracious and effective so that you will have the right answer for everyone." Colossians 4:5,6

INTEREST

Remember that salvation is a work of God. If a person shows no interest just let it go. Nobody can drag a person to Christ and we can't force people into the kingdom. If God has already been working in a person's heart, you will sense a curiosity and interest in spiritual things. They will want to hear the good news. And you can cooperate with God to share the good news with them.

"There are different ways God works in our lives, but it is the same God who does the work through all of us." 1 Corinthians 12:6

MAKE A FRIEND

As we reach out to people that are far from God, remember that people will listen to a friend more quickly than they will a stranger. Make a friend first. People won't care how much you know until they know how much you care. If you can, find out something about the person with whom you are sharing the good news. Help them realize that you are not pushing religion, you are sharing with them truth that is essential for every person in the world.

"The heartfelt counsel of a friend is as sweet as perfume and incense." Proverbs 27:9

POINT OF NEED

Simply put, God offers at least three things in salvation through the death of Christ:
1. Forgiveness for our sins (Freedom from failure and guilt)
2. Power to live a new life (Freedom from dependency and uncontrollable behavior)
3. Assurance of heaven (Freedom from fear of death and loss of loved ones)

Everyone you talk to that does not know Christ will have a need in one of these areas. Often spiritual conversations can lead you to their point of need. We do not have to solve people's problems, but we can point them to the Christ who can. We can also tell people with great needs that we will pray for them.

"When Jesus heard this, he told them, "Healthy people don't need a doctor — sick people do. I have come to call sinners, not those who think they are already good enough." Mark 2:17

TELLING YOUR STORY

The best thing you can include in sharing the good news is how it happened to you. The testimony of the apostle Paul is recorded three times in the New Testament. I am sure he shared it every time he got to talk to someone. How did you come to know Jesus Christ as your personal Savior? Telling your story is irrefutable. Nobody can say to you, "That isn't true, I don't believe that." Because you are sharing what actually happened to you. If you have never told your story, don't worry about it being impressive or dramatic. Keep it simple. Just get a piece of paper and write it out including these three things;

    1. What it was like before you knew about Christ.

    2. The circumstances and truths that brought you to Him. (Use a scripture verse)

    3. How Christ has changed your life since you trusted Him as your Savior.

SHARING THE GOSPEL

Once someone shows some interest in the plaque, you can begin telling the great story of God's rescue of fallen mankind. You should use your own words but this is just one way you can explain it as you point out the different elements in the drawing. The words in BOLD indicate the main thought for that section and a key scripture verse. The bullets (•) are the specific illustrations you can point to as you explain them. The scripture references that follow in parentheses ( ) are additional verses from the Bible to give greater meaning to what you are saying.

1. GOD SO LOVED THE WORLD -

"For God so loved the world that he gave his only Son…" John 3:16

"This is a wonderful drawing because it tells the story of how much God loves us. It starts here with the birth of Christ in Bethlehem. It was a special birth because it was God's own son being born."

- You can see the star that appeared over the stable. (Matthew 2:2)
- Here is Mary who was told by an angel that she would fulfill the prophecy
  in the book of Isaiah that spoke of a virgin bearing a child. (Isaiah 7:14)
- This is Joseph who also got word from God that He was showing his love for us
  by calling this child Emmanuel translated "God with us". (Matthew 1:20-23)
- The manger by the ox and lamb where the baby was placed. (Luke 2:6,7)

2. GOOD NEWS: GOD IS GOING TO RESCUE PEOPLE FROM THEIR SINS!

"… name him Jesus, for he will save his people from their sins." Matthew 1:21

"The word 'gospel' means 'good news'! The angels and the shepherds were excited because God was fulfilling a long-standing promise that the Lamb of God would cleanse people of the guilt of their sin. (Isaiah 53:6,7)

- On the hillside of Judea were the Shepherds who heard the announcement of
  great joy for everyone (Luke 2:8-10)
- Angels announced His birth, offering glory to God and peace to all men.
  (Luke 2:13,14)

3. JESUS IS THE WAY

"I am the way, the truth and the life, no one can come to the Father except through me."
John 14:6

"When Jesus grew up and began teaching, His message to the world was a radical one. He began teaching that all people could find forgiveness, freedom and eternal life only through Him."

- Christ began teaching the people that He was the fulfillment of hundreds of prophecies contained in the Hebrew writings that pointed only to Him. He read from the book of Isaiah that the time of the Lord's favor had come. (Isaiah 61:1,2, Luke 4:16)
- He called His disciples from their fishing boats on the Sea of Galilee and told them that they could become fishers of men. (Matthew 4:19)

4. JESUS OFFERS THE BREAD OF LIFE

"I assure you, anyone who believes in me already has eternal life. Yes, I am the bread of life!" John 6:48

Everybody on earth who is alive knows that something in life is missing. Nothing is ever completely perfect. Everybody eventually has problems and eventually is going to die. What Jesus came to offer was a different kind of life. He offers you abundant life here on earth and eternal life in heaven. Jesus Christ is the solution to the problems in this life and the ultimate answer to death.

- A young boy understood that Jesus was not an ordinary man and offered him his picnic lunch of a few loaves of bread and fish. (Matt. 14:15-21, Mark 6:35-42, Luke 9:12-17)
- Jesus took what the boy had given Him and transformed it into an abundance for the hungry crowd. It was after this miracle that Peter understood that Jesus was the chosen one sent by God. (John 6:37)

5. A PRAYER FOR YOU

"I am praying not only for these disciples but also for all who will ever believe in me because of their testimony." John 17:20

Jesus prayed for you. As God, Jesus knows everything about you and wants you to trust Him as your savior. He is interested in a personal relationship with you.

- Christ is praying in the Garden of Gethsemane. He is preparing to take your sins and the sins of the whole world upon Himself to set you free from that burden. (John 17:9-21)

6. HIS WILLING SACRIFICE

"No one takes my life from me. I lay down my life voluntarily. For I have the right to lay it down when I want to and also the power to take it again." John 10:18

Jesus was not dragged to the cross against His will. He gave His life for you willingly because of His great love for you. If you were the only person on the face of the earth that needed salvation, Christ would have died for you.

- The road to Calvary where Jesus carried His cross was taken voluntarily. (Philippians 2:6-11)

7. PAID IN FULL

"He paid for you with the precious lifeblood of Christ, the sinless, spotless Lamb of God." 1 Peter 1:19

The last word Jesus said on the cross was "tetelestai" translated "It is finished." The phrase would be better rendered "paid in full." Outstanding debts during the time of Christ were stamped with the Greek word "tetelestai" which meant this debt had been satisfied. It had been paid. The debt of our sin was completely paid for by the death of Christ on the Cross. By faith in that sacrifice we are forgiven.

- Christ hung on the cross in our place. (2 Corinthians 5:21)
- His death set us free from all our failures and sins. (Romans 6:7)

8. FACING OUR DOUBTS

"When they saw him, they worshiped him—but some of them still doubted!" Matthew 28:17

After the death of Christ many of His followers gave up hope and went home. As Jesus was being prepared for His burial, even Mary his mother experienced doubts about the promises He had made. Thomas, one of the twelve boldly proclaimed "Unless I see the scars of the nails in His hands I will not believe." It is natural to have doubts about the divinity of Christ and the salvation He offers. Especially in our modern culture many unbelievers scoff at Christ's claims of being the Savior of the world.

- Mary was afraid and doubted the truth of Christ's claims. (Mary and the apostles doubted, - Luke 24:38, Thomas doubted - John 20:26-28, Peter doubted - Matthew 14:31)

9. POWERFUL EVIDENCE

"the fact is that Christ has been raised from the dead. He has become the first of a great harvest of those who will be raised to life again." 1 Corinthians 15:20

Yes, the fact is that Christ was raised from the dead! In him we can also look forward to life in heaven after death. It is the empty tomb that gives us the confirmation of all that

Christ promised. To this day no skeptic can explain away the empty tomb. Not only was the tomb found empty but Christ appeared to over four hundred of His followers in the forty days following His resurrection.

- It is in the empty tomb that we can lay our doubts and fears to rest. (Acts 1:3)
- Because Jesus is alive after His death we can know that we also will live with him forever. (2 Corinthians 4:14)

10. IS HE YOUR SAVIOR?

"Furthermore, we have seen with our own eyes and now testify that the Father sent his Son to be the Savior of the world." 1 John 4:14

And so we return to the manger and the claim made by the angels that this child named Jesus would be the Savior of the world. The rest of the verse that we started with in this drawing was John 3:16 where Christ Himself makes a proposition; "whoever believes in me shall not perish but have everlasting life." (John 3:16) As simply as it can be put, if you will trust in Jesus, God will give you a great gift of freedom:

- Freedom from the past; Forgiveness from the guilt of failures and sins. (Romans 5:15)
- Freedom to live a new life; The Power to have victory over the failures in your life. (Romans 6:22)
- Freedom from the fear of death; The promise of eternal life! (Romans 6:23)

CLOSING

At this point in your explanation of the Gospel using the drawing of the Face of Christ it is very appropriate to turn to the person you are speaking to and ask a question or two.

- "Have you ever heard this explained before?"
- "Does it make sense to you?"
- "Would you be willing to trust in Christ as your Savior?"
  If they answer "yes" then you can say "Would you be willing to pray with me right now?" And then you can lead them in this prayer out loud or they can pray it silently as you speak the words.

"Dear Father in heaven, thank you for sending your son Jesus to die in my place. I realize that I have failed you and that I need forgiveness. In this moment I place my faith in Jesus your son trusting him alone for my salvation. I believe that you have removed the guilt of my sin. Help me live the kind of life you want me to live in the power of your spirit. Thank you for the assurance of eternal life in heaven with you. Amen"

God assures us that faith in Christ transforms us into forgiven, victorious, eternal beings. You can share that confidence with those who have prayed with you by sharing some of these verses:

"God has purchased our freedom with his blood and has forgiven all our sins."
   Colossians 1:14

"What this means is that those who become Christians become new persons. They are not the same anymore, for the old life is gone. A new life has begun!"
   2 Corinthians 5:17

"I write this to you who believe in the Son of God, so that you may know you have eternal life." 1 John 5:13

FINAL THOUGHTS

People who come to Christ arrive as spiritual children who need encouragement, prayer and direction for their new life. It is important to give these new believers some important information to help them continue the process of becoming a disciple of Jesus. Here is a short list of the essentials.

- Purchase a Bible and read it daily. It gives strength, wisdom and Spiritual Food. (1 Peter 2:2, Hebrews 5:12,13)
- Begin talking to God in prayer. God is now our spiritual father and longs to for us to know Him. (Matthew 6:6-9, Matthew 26:41)
- Get involved in a good church that believes and teaches the Bible. It is important to find a place where you will fit in and find spiritual fellowship and nourishment. (Acts 14:27, Hebrews 10:25)
- Use your resources, talents and abilities for the Savior. (Luke 16:9-12)
- Share the good news with others who need to hear it. (Luke 5:10, 1 Corinthians 9:23)

In closing, I would encourage you to pray for those who have come into the kingdom because of your faithfulness. Stay in touch with them if possible and help them become mature disciples who also become active in sharing the good news with others.

I would very much like to hear the stories of these who have been impacted using the 'Face of Christ' drawing. Please write or e-mail us and share your stories. I would feel honored to pray for you and those with whom you share. You can read more stories and see more of my drawings at my web site ArtStonePublishers.com

May God bless your efforts

Joe Castillo
artstone@artstonepublishers.com